FORGETTING YOU

LOVE SONGS

SIDHARTH PK

Copyright © Sidharth Pk
All Rights Reserved.

This book has been published with all efforts taken to make the material error-free after the consent of the author. However, the author and the publisher do not assume and hereby disclaim any liability to any party for any loss, damage, or disruption caused by errors or omissions, whether such errors or omissions result from negligence, accident, or any other cause.

While every effort has been made to avoid any mistake or omission, this publication is being sold on the condition and understanding that neither the author nor the publishers or printers would be liable in any manner to any person by reason of any mistake or omission in this publication or for any action taken or omitted to be taken or advice rendered or accepted on the basis of this work. For any defect in printing or binding the publishers will be liable only to replace the defective copy by another copy of this work then available.

To a young beautiful girl, who is gone forever.

Contents

Foreword   *vii*

Preface   *ix*

Acknowledgements   *xi*

1. Forgetting You   1

2. To A Morning Star   2

3. Come Realize Your Dreams   3

4. Up In A Mountain Top   4

5. This Moonlight   5

6. The Twlight   6

7. The Call Of The Night   7

8. Don't Drag Your Feet   8

To Be Continued   9

Foreword

The poems in this collection speaks out about the beauty and splendour of the universe. The poet has tried to capture the beauty of the ravishing night and dazzling of the world into verses. The poet uses rich imagery to create an lasting impact.

This short but splendid collection of poetry that throws light on the beauty of the nature at a large.

Preface

This book is a reflection of my love for nature. I managed to bring your kind azttention to the splendour of the universe and the world. Poems in this book opines to give a picture on the rich beauty of the world and the night. stars and the moon at large. I kindly present this book to my young readers.

sidharth pk

Mg university, Ma: History

Kottayam

Acknowledgements

I thank all the brains who worked behind me in shaping of this book. I express my inmost gratitude to all who helped me in forming this creative work.

Thank you all.

1. Forgetting You

The breeze plays with your sleek cascade,
I long not forgetting you
I found the beauty of the moon
In your blushing eyes,
Like the eyes of starry quality.
The world will look so bleak,
Dull and anguish without you
The fever of love and forgetting
Will meet too- soon
Silence and tears will abide you.
Love is crushed like a flower,
It's crumbled like a leafy plant
I believe that it was
Destiny that showed me, you
Our love will be painted in blood.

2. To a Morning Star

The blue skies shimmers,
I see a star, in the Heaven's high
I dream to touch it
Fly to you.
The morning's blessings and,
The horizon bright in hue
Birds in full throated
Sings a doleful strain.
Come, oh silver dawn,
The dawn of calmness
Let the torch of love
Be kindled.

3. Come Realize Your Dreams

The silver dawn shoots up the blue sky,
Come realise your dreams, here
In this hollowed spot
And let light be your wisdom.
The azure has wrapped the universe,
In the blanket of hope
A new beginning for all
Start from where you are now.
Small birds loitter in the garden,
Earth welcomes the ray of hope
From the close bosoming friend sun
And start your journey.

4. Up in a Mountain Top

I hear a voice far away,
A distant vibrating sound
Soft voice, singing a air
The wind carries it forth.
See how the mountain tops touch,
The heaven's high dome
Sun is mellowed in the light
And charms the world.

5. This Moonlight

This moonlight will die,
And love too will fade
What is left for us?
In this world, is unknown?
The moon beams love,
And the stars shine in glee
And the moon yet goes into mystery,
Into the silence of the night.

6. The Twlight

The dusky twilight fair,
Meet in her eyes
And the moonless air
The bright starry skies
Yet are manifestations
of her charms and beauty.
The evening in purple and glow,
Night without the moon
Magic in you flow
We will meet too- soon
As the night remains starry
And the constellation is young.

7. The Call of The Night

The moon shines brightly in the universe,
And the stars glow in the milky way
Creating a gentle casting constellation
Night charms the world.
In the western hemisphere, a star
Is gently seen beaming
The light of the moon
Is blue and splendid.
How beautiful the world is to be seen?
The night calls me
And moves into darkness
Expire in the night's mystery.

8. Don't Drag Your Feet

Don't drag your feet,
In the sands of time
Your feedt makes a musical note
Sweet to hear.
Leave your mark here,
Leave your foot print
In the sands of time
And tread softly.

To Be Continued

continued.......

www.ingramcontent.com/pod-product-compliance
Lightning Source LLC
Chambersburg PA
CBHW060234170726
48004CB00004BA/1536